Tiger's Drum Kit

Jan Burchett and Sara Vogler
Illustrated by Jon Stuart

OXFORD

In this story ...

Tiger

Toby

Tiger's Mum

Tiger's Dad

Tiger had a new drum kit.
He liked to play it loud.

Toby was cross. He had to turn up the TV.

Tiger took his drums to the kitchen.
Dad put his fingers in his ears.
"What a noise!" he said.

Tiger took his drums into his bedroom.
"What a noise!" said Mum.

“Where can I play my drums?” thought Tiger.
Then he had an idea.

He got bottle tops, metal lids and bits of wire. He put them in his cupboard. Then he pushed the button on his watch …

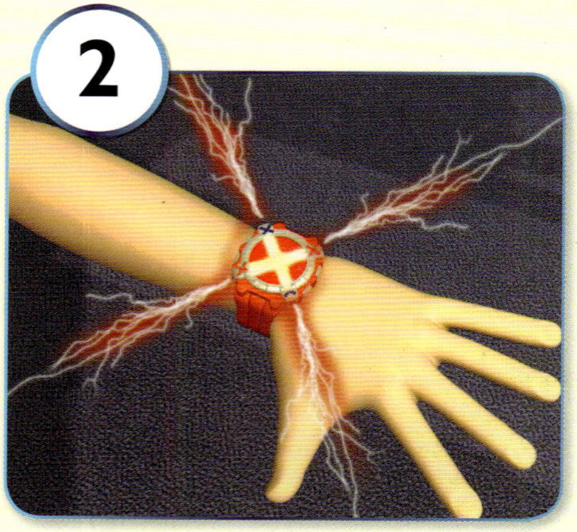

Tiger went into the cupboard.
He made himself a new drum kit.

He banged and bashed his new drum kit. No one heard a thing. "Cool!" grinned Tiger.

Suddenly Mum came in. She took some sheets out of the cupboard and shut the door. Tiger was trapped!

Tiger tried to push the cupboard door open. He shouted. He bashed two tin lids together. No one heard a thing.

Then Tiger lifted up part of a drum.
He banged it down hard on a pipe.
Bang! Bang! BANG!
"What a noise!" said Tiger.

The sound went along the pipe.
It went round the whole house.
"What's that noise?" asked Mum.
"What is Tiger up to now?"

They followed the noise to Tiger's room. Tiger was not there. Dad opened the cupboard. Tiger was not there. "Where is Tiger?" said Mum.

“Here I am,” said Tiger. “What is all the noise?”